HARRY HOUDINI

The Legend of the World's Greatest Escape Artist

BY

Janice Weaver

ILLUSTRATIONS

Chris Lane

Abrams Books for Young Readers
New York

Cataloging-in-Publication Data has been applied for and may be obtained from the
Library of Congress.

ISBN: 978-1-4197-0014-9

Harry Houdini: The Legend of the World's Greatest Escape Artist was produced by
Madison Press Books
1000 Yonge Street, Suite 303
Toronto, Ontario
Canada M4W 2K2
www.madisonpressbooks.com

Printed and bound in China
10 9 8 7 6 5 4 3 2 1

Abrams Books for Young Readers are available at special discounts when purchased in quantity for
premiums and promotions as well as fundraising or educational use. Special editions can also be
created to specification. For details, contact specialsales@abramsbooks.com or the address below.

▲
Abrams Books
for Young Readers
115 West 18th Street
New York, NY 10011
www.abramsbooks.com

CONTENTS

GROWING UP

Flying through the air with perhaps not quite the greatest of ease, the young boy in the handmade red woolen tights put on an astonishing show for those who'd gathered for his friend Jack Hoeffler's small sandlot circus. Calling himself Ehrich, Prince of the Air, the boy swung from ropes and tumbled across the stony field and twisted himself into unusual shapes to impress and amaze. He even—or so he later claimed—bent over backward to pick up a pin from the ground with his eyelashes.

The boy had been inspired by a tightrope walker he'd seen when the traveling circus came through town. While the man had inched his way across the narrow wire, the audience sat spellbound in the stands below, too anxious to move or even breathe. The man had no harness to hold him and no net to catch him if he fell. When he at last made it safely to the other side, the crowd roared with both wonder and relief.

It was the most amazing thing the boy had ever seen, and he knew he had to do something like it too.

☞ ☜

Ehrich Weiss, the boy who would become Harry Houdini, was born on March 24, 1874, in Budapest, the vibrant capital city of Hungary. Budapest was a beautiful, cosmopolitan place, a center of culture and business.

RIGHT: Ehrich, Prince of the Air

Harry's father, Mayer Weiss, and his infant son, Armin, had moved there from the countryside after the death of Mayer's first wife, and it was there that he met Cecilia Steiner, a beautiful young woman who would become his second wife and the mother of Harry and his five siblings.

Harry's father, like so many others, was drawn to Budapest because of its prosperity and its reputation for tolerance. The Weisses were Jewish, and in those days, Jewish people were often prevented from living in certain areas and working at some professions. Hungary was more accepting than many European countries, though, and had passed laws that gave Jewish people the same rights and privileges as all other citizens. Because of this, Jews who were discriminated against or mistreated in other parts of Europe flocked to Budapest, helping to turn it into a thriving, exciting city.

For some reason, however, Harry's father wasn't able to take advantage of the opportunities Budapest offered. Although he was intelligent and well educated—he had a doctorate and a law degree, was a rabbi, and spoke several languages—he struggled to earn a decent living. When a friend in America suggested that he emigrate, he wasted no time in deciding to go. Leaving his pregnant wife and by then four sons behind, he set off for tiny Appleton, Wisconsin, to take up a position as the rabbi of the town's only temple.

Finally, things seemed to go well for Rabbi Weiss. The members of the congregation liked him and treated him with the respect he'd always craved. After two years there, he felt secure enough in his position to send for his wife and children. Four-year-old Harry, his mother, and his brothers Armin, Natan, Gottfried Vilmos, and Dezso (the baby, who'd yet to meet his father) set sail for New York on June 19, 1878. They had only enough money to pay for passage in steerage—the cheapest tickets available—which meant they had to endure two weeks of travel in noisy, dark conditions, crammed in with hundreds of other passengers. But it was a small price to pay for the chance at a new life in America.

ABOVE: Idyllic Appleton, Wisconsin, on the banks of the Fox River.
RIGHT: The postcard the young runaway sent his worried mother.
BELOW: Harry (left), at about age three, places a protective arm around his baby brother, Dash.

To Harry, Appleton was a magical place to grow up. The bustling little town sat on the banks of the winding Fox River and was surrounded by thick pine woods that provided the lumber for the local paper mills, the source of much of the town's employment. There were towering trees to climb, wide boulevards to run along, and muddy riverbanks to explore. For a curious and adventuresome boy like Harry, there was no better place to be.

But these idyllic times did not last. In 1882, Mayer Weiss was fired by his synagogue when the members of the congregation decided they wanted a more modern rabbi. "One morning," Harry later wrote of this great blow, "my father awoke to find himself thrown upon the world, his long locks of hair having silvered in service, with seven children to feed, without a position, and without any visible means of support."

This was the start of a very difficult period in the life of the Weisses. They moved to nearby Milwaukee, a bigger city where opportunities should have been easier to come by. But even there, Harry remembered, they found nothing except "hardships and hunger." All the children were put to work to help make ends meet, with now eight-year-old Harry selling newspapers, running errands, and shining shoes in front of the city's grandest hotel. But every day was a struggle even to find enough to eat. The children went to school only occasionally, and for the next four years, the family moved from one small apartment to another, trying to stay one step ahead of the debt collector.

In these tough times, Harry knew he had to grow up fast. He wanted to get out into the world to seek his fortune and then come home to help his family. Packing up his shoeshine kit, an armload of books, and a deck of cards, he hopped a train, planning to follow the U.S. cavalry as they helped open up the western frontier. "I am going to Galveston, Texas," he wrote in a postcard he sent his mother, "and will be back in about a year." He was just twelve years old.

COMING TO AMERICA

Harry, his mother, and his brothers came into the United States through the Castle Garden immigration station, a former sandstone fortress at the very tip of Manhattan. This was the main point of entry for immigrants to America before Ellis Island opened in 1892.

Castle Garden was organized into a series of departments. These included the information department, where staff helped immigrants connect with friends and relatives who'd come to meet them; the labor exchange, where newcomers could find work in trades like shoemaking and baking; and the letter-writing department, where translators wrote notes and documents in any number of languages for the new arrivals, who often couldn't read and write. Immigrants were also checked for signs of illness and given assistance in finding lodgings, and clerks in the registering department interviewed each one, recording their names, nationalities, and end destinations.

As part of this interview process, people from non-English-speaking countries were often given new "Americanized" names. In the case of the Weisses, Harry's brother Armin became Herman; Natan became Nathan; Gottfried Vilmos became William; and the baby, Dezso, became Theo (and was later nicknamed "Dash"). Harry, who was called Erik at birth, became Ehrich, and the whole family's name was changed from Weisz to Weiss.

Castle Garden was praised as "a great national refuge for immigrants from all lands." In the thirty-four years it was used as a landing depot, at least eight million people passed through its doors on their way to a new life in America.

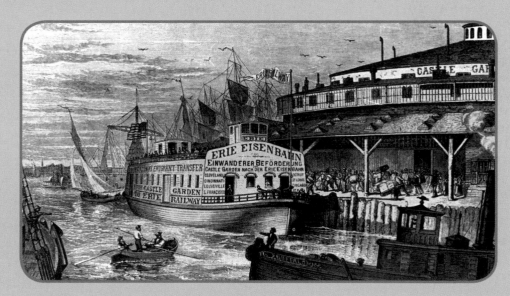

ABOVE: A boatload of newly arrived immigrants prepare to make their way to Castle Garden, the round building in the background, for processing.

ABRACADABRA

Harry never made it to Galveston. Instead, he settled in nearby Delavan, Wisconsin, where a kindly older couple took him in, fed him, bathed him, and offered him a great soft bed. While Harry was off on this grand adventure, his father also left the family behind, moving to New York to look for work. In 1887, Harry joined him there, and father and son shared a small room in a boardinghouse while they tried to get on their feet. Mayer Weiss was earning some money giving Hebrew lessons and cutting cloth for a garment factory, but it wasn't nearly enough to make ends meet. Although he was still only thirteen, Harry had to chip in too. He quickly found work delivering messages for a telegraph company.

Within a year, Harry and his father had earned enough to rent a proper apartment and send for the rest of the family. But the tough times were still not behind them. Winter arrived, and the Weisses found they couldn't afford coal to heat their modest home. They got behind on their rent and struggled again to pay their bills and put food on the table.

Although Harry's father was a good man, he sometimes had difficulty facing his problems. He liked to believe that some miracle would happen to make them all go away. Fortunately, his son was more sensible and more enterprising. On this occasion, Harry realized that the Christmas season had put New Yorkers in a generous mood. He set off for work the next day wearing a sign that read:

RIGHT: Harry the messenger boy

CHILD LABOR

It wasn't unusual in the 1800s and early 1900s for children like Harry to take jobs to try to help their families make ends meet. In the United States, Britain, Canada, and most other countries around the world, children worked as errand boys, match girls, chimney sweeps, and shoe shiners. In more rural areas, many went down into the coal mines, where their small size allowed them to crawl into spots too tight for adults to reach. And in the cities, thousands ended up like Harry, working in the grubby and often dangerous factories that had sprung up during the Industrial Revolution.

People's attitudes toward child labor finally began to change in the 1930s. New laws, including the U.S. Fair Labor Standards Act, were passed to protect children from dangerous working conditions. But what made the biggest difference was the Great Depression. That calamity made men and women so desperate for work that they were willing to do the jobs children had once done.

A necktie factory similar to the one in which Houdini worked.

Christmas is coming,
Turkeys are fat.
Please drop a quarter
In the messenger boy's hat.

That did the trick! All day long people read Harry's sign with amusement and did as he asked, dropping money in his hat. Before he got home that night, he gathered all the coins he'd collected and hid them anywhere he could think of—up his sleeves, behind his ears, in the cuffs of his pants. When he walked in the door, he said to his mother, "Shake me. I'm magic!" Not sure what to think, Mrs. Weiss lifted her young son and started shaking, and as she did, out tumbled a cascade of coins—enough to pay off the landlord and save the family from eviction.

☞ ☜

Like many young people of the time, Harry didn't have much formal education. But he made up for what he lacked with creativity, resourcefulness, and the cunning he'd learned on the streets. When he left his job as a messenger boy, these were exactly the qualities that helped him find something better.

Walking past a necktie factory one day, Harry noticed a sign advertising a job for an assistant cutter. These were tough times in America, and a long line of job seekers had already formed. Harry knew he had no hope if he just lined up behind everyone else, so he swallowed hard, squared his shoulders, and strode to the front with purpose. Turning to address the crowd, he thanked the men for coming and told them the position had been filled. Then he picked up the sign and strolled inside to claim the job for himself.

At the tie factory, Harry quickly made friends with another young cutter named Jacob Hyman. Jacob and Harry discovered a shared love of magic, and they spent their breaks at the factory practicing simple tricks with cards and coins. But Harry already had his mind on bigger things. He had stumbled across a book by Jean Eugène Robert-Houdin, then one of the most famous magicians in the world, and it had already started to change his life.

The Memoirs of Robert-Houdin was the story of the great entertainer's incredible life and career. He wrote of learning the tricks of his trade from an old magician who took him under his wing, and of becoming so successful that he performed for the kings and queens of Europe. He described the fantastic illusions for which he was most famous—making people float in midair, for example, or causing orange trees to sprout fruit right before an audience's eyes. It was the most amazing book Harry had ever read. It "gave the [magic] profession a dignity worth attaining at the cost of earnest, lifelong effort," he later recalled. "From the moment I began to study the art, [Robert-Houdin] became my guide and my hero. I accepted his writings as my textbook and my gospel."

In a courageous and foolhardy move, Harry—convinced that there was more to life than cutting fabric in a tie factory—left his job for what he was sure would be bright lights and great success. He and Jacob Hyman formed a magic act, billing themselves as the Modern Monarchs of Mystery. "I asked nothing more of life than to become in my profession 'like Robert-Houdin,'" Houdini remembered. When Jacob told him, mistakenly, that adding the letter *i* to Houdin's name would mean, in French, "like Houdin," Harry "adopted the suggestion with enthusiasm."

Gone was Ehrich Weiss. Harry Houdini was born.

☜ ☞

Just as Harry was beginning to find his way in the world, his father became ill with cancer. As the old man lay near death, he called his son to his bedside and had him promise to look after his mother. Although Harry wasn't the oldest child, Mayer Weiss clearly thought he had the energy and intensity to succeed. Even without a formal education or a regular paycheck, Harry vowed to do as his dying father asked.

ABOVE: Houdini's idol, the great Robert-Houdin. BELOW: Early in his career, Harry billed himself as the King of Cards.

To fulfill his promise, Harry took whatever magic bookings he could find. He and Jacob Hyman had a polished but unexceptional act based on some simple sleight-of-hand, including card and handkerchief tricks. They performed everywhere they could—in small circuses, at fairs and carnivals, and in tiny theaters in the tiniest of towns.

This was a tough way to make a living, though. Harry and Jacob often performed a dozen or more shows a day, usually for less than a dollar each. The carnivals and circus sideshows were bleak places that appealed to the poorest of the poor, and the people on display were the most marginalized in society. Maybe it was all too much for Jacob Hyman. He and Harry argued and eventually fell out, and he left the act in 1894.

But Harry was never one to stay down for long. He replaced Jacob with his brother Dash and changed the name of the act to the Houdini Brothers. Using Dash's entire life savings—twenty-five dollars he'd worked hard to save—the brothers bought some new equipment, as well as the right to perform a trick called the Substitution Trunk.

In this trick, Harry would bind Dash's hands behind his back, then tie him in a canvas sack. Once secured, Dash was placed inside a large trunk, which was then locked and tied with ropes. While Harry promised the audience they were about to witness a miracle, a curtain was pulled around the trunk to hide it from view. Stepping behind the curtain, Harry clapped his hands three times and—*Presto!*—out stepped Dash. The younger brother then pulled aside the curtain, opened the still-locked trunk, and untied the sack to reveal Harry now inside, his hands bound just as Dash's had been only moments before.

The brothers renamed the trick Metamorphosis, a word that means "transformation." It was a fitting title, for this trick would eventually help transform Harry from a run-of-the-mill sleight-of-hand man to a magician unlike any the world had ever seen.

LEFT: The young magician shows off some of the tricks of his trade.

HOW DID THEY DO IT?

Metamorphosis was actually a simple trick that relied entirely on speed and agility. As soon as Dash was shut in the trunk, he would free his hands from the rope, keeping the knot intact. Next, he'd wriggle out of the sack through a slit in the bottom—shouting and banging away the whole time for the greatest dramatic impact. And finally, he would escape the trunk itself through a trapdoor in its side. Once Dash was free, Harry would reverse the process, crawling back into the trunk through the trapdoor and squirming into the sack through the hole in the bottom. When the trunk was opened, the knot at the top of the sack was undisturbed, and it looked to all the world as if the brothers had switched places by supernatural means.

Eventually, Harry and Dash were able to complete the trick in just three seconds. Audience members were amazed at their ability to switch places with lightning-like, almost unearthly speed.

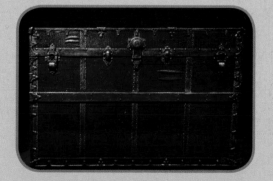

The supposedly escape-proof trunk from Harry and Dash's Metamorphosis trick.

TAKING CENTER STAGE

In the spring of 1894, Harry and Dash got a job working at Coney Island, a beachside amusement park at the mouth of New York Harbor. Coney Island was famous for its boardwalk, its roller coasters and carousels, and its sideshows and other low-cost attractions. New Yorkers flocked there during the summer to escape the heat of their crowded city.

The hall where the Houdini Brothers performed also hosted several other entertainers, including a song-and-dance act called the Floral Sisters. One of the girls in the act was a beautiful eighteen-year-old named Wilhelmina Beatrice Rahner, known as Bess to her friends. Harry and Bess took one look at each other and fell instantly, madly in love. Just three short weeks later, they announced to family and friends that they had gotten married.

In Bess, Harry found both a life partner and a new partner for his act. She was a tiny woman—less than five feet tall and under a hundred pounds—which made her a natural for squeezing in and out of the trunk in the Metamorphosis trick. And it turned out that audiences were more interested in a husband-and-wife magic act than one with two brothers. Dash bowed out and moved on to start a new show of his own.

The Houdinis worked hard, performing as many as ten or twenty times a day at carnivals and town fairs and in rough storefront halls called dime museums. They usually earned less than twenty dollars a week, which

RIGHT: Bess, the great love of Houdini's life

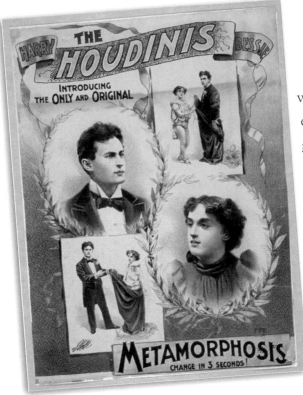

was barely enough to get by on, even though they sometimes got free meals as well. They spent weeks at a time on the road, working in one small town and then moving on to the next.

At one point, Harry and Bess got a six-month job with a traveling circus in Pennsylvania. They were required to do whatever the boss asked of them, from their magic act to a mind-reading routine to a Punch-and-Judy puppet show. Harry sometimes made up his face, tousled his hair, and dressed himself in burlap sacks to pretend to be Projea, the Wild Man of Mexico, and Bess occasionally had to work as a singing clown. In the evenings, they retired to their living quarters, which consisted of a narrow cot in the back of an old freight train, where a thin curtain was all that separated them from the other performers.

When their contract was up, the Houdinis were back to taking short-term, low-paying jobs at fairs and carnivals. Harry managed to lose what little money they'd saved by investing it in a shady business deal. To recover from that loss, he and Bess signed on with a magic troupe that was going to tour New Brunswick and Nova Scotia. In the Maritimes, their Metamorphosis trick was well received, but the show itself suffered from poor ticket sales and eventually went bankrupt. The Houdinis were out of work once more.

This wasn't much of a life for a young couple just starting out. Jobs were scarce, and money was even scarcer. In 1898, Harry became so

LEFT: This poster advertising the Metamorphosis trick boasts that the switch can be made in just three seconds. ABOVE: Harry and Bess, during their first year as husband and wife.

18

discouraged that he contemplated quitting show business altogether to try opening a school of magic in New York. When that idea also failed to take off, he offered to sell all his secrets—a magician's whole stock in trade—to the newspapers for twenty dollars. Even then he couldn't stir up any interest in his act.

Still, these lean and difficult years weren't a complete waste. All those daily performances made Harry adept at handling an audience, which he knew was what separated the good magicians from the bad. All the card tricks and other bits of sleight-of-hand gave him nimble fingers that were perfect for picking locks. And all his fellow performers taught him new skills—including how to untie knots with his toes, and how to swallow something and then cough it back up again—that would come in handy in his future career as the world's greatest escape artist.

He had all the pieces he needed. Now he just had to put the puzzle together.

☞ ☜

Throughout the winter and spring of 1898 and 1899, the Houdinis performed at beer halls, small theaters, and dime museums throughout the American Midwest. By now, their act was a mix of well-worn card and handkerchief tricks and the Metamorphosis escape. It was a reliable routine, but it lacked originality. It was never going to raise Harry above the ranks of all the other traveling magicians of the day.

One night, after an appearance at a beer hall in Minnesota, Harry and Bess were approached by an elegant-looking man with a thick German accent. When this well-dressed stranger pronounced their show an unfocused disaster, Houdini probably took quick offense. Although he always claimed to look upon criticism as "a friendly favor," Harry actually had extremely thin skin and was often badly hurt by people's

THE DIME MUSEUMS

The "dime museums" where Harry got his start were at the low end of the entertainment industry. They were small storefront stages that featured human curiosities—people who looked different or had something unusual about them—in what were often unkindly called "freak shows." For just a dime admission, visitors could tour the stages to gawk at bearded ladies, Siamese twins, and dog-faced men. In the days before movies and television, this was one of the most common forms of popular entertainment.

The dime museums also had other attractions, like waxworks and magic shows, and sometimes they displayed exotic animals or scientific or medical instruments. The most famous of the dime museums was P.T. Barnum's American Museum in New York City. At the height of its popularity, as many as fifteen thousand people went through its doors each day.

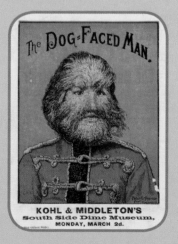

An advertisement for the Dog-Faced Man at the South Side Dime Museum in Chicago.

comments about his act. This was no exception. Who was this man to say such things?

In fact, the man was Martin Beck, a successful promoter and the manager of the Orpheum theaters, a chain known for paying its performers very well. Beck told Houdini that he should drop all his ordinary tricks—the ones found in any magician's repertoire—and instead focus on those that set him apart: the trunk trick and some handcuff escapes he'd started trying. If he did that, Beck said, he had a spot on the Orpheum circuit.

Before Houdini could say "Abracadabra," he and Bess were on a train headed for Beck's theater in San Francisco, and a whole new way of life. Beck had convinced Harry of the value of doing a few tricks with great dramatic flair, and that in turn had given the young magician a brilliant new idea: He added a twist to his handcuff escapes by inviting members of the public to bring their own cuffs and shackles to the theater to challenge him. Anyone who produced a set of restraints from which he couldn't escape would win a hundred dollars, no small sum for its time.

The Challenge Handcuff Escape was a great bit of showmanship because it gave the audience a stake in the outcome of the act. Harry had finally learned that a magician's success was based not so much on what he did onstage but on how he connected with the people who'd come to watch him. "Don't think that because you perform a trick well . . . you have conquered the world of mystery," he later wrote. The real trick lay in conquering the audience.

And conquer he did. Night after night, Houdini performed his new act to packed houses of admiring fans, creating, in his own words, "the biggest sensation in California since the discovery of gold in 1849." Beck couldn't have been happier. He raised Harry's salary to $90 a week, then again to $125, and finally to $250, ten times what Harry had been earning just a few months earlier. Now, the vaudeville impresario said, it was time for Houdini to take his talent overseas.

TOP: In 1900, Houdini took his handcuff act to Europe, where he was a huge success. BOTTOM: Brother Dash (left) was invited overseas to enjoy the spoils.

"**Most of my success in Europe** was due to the fact that I lost no time in stirring up local interest in every town I played," Houdini later wrote. "The first thing was to break out of jail."

For months, he'd been attracting interest in his act by dropping by the local police station in each new city he visited and challenging the officers to lock him up in their most secure cuffs and cell. Each successful escape—and they were *all* successful—helped spread his reputation. Now he made a beeline for the famous headquarters of the London police, Scotland Yard, to do it again.

Heading straight for the top, Harry met with William Melville, the superintendent of police, and asked to be restrained as if he were one of Scotland Yard's most-wanted criminals. The ever-accommodating London bobby immediately grabbed Houdini's arms, wrapped them around a nearby pillar, and chained his wrists with several pairs of handcuffs.

"These aren't stage handcuffs," Melville warned. "They're how we fasten Yankee criminals who come over here and get into trouble." As he started for the door, he added smugly, "I'll come back for you in a couple of hours."

"Wait!" said Houdini, turning from the pillar and dropping the opened handcuffs in an embarrassing heap upon the floor. "I'll go with you."

It had taken him only seconds to free himself.

Houdini's masterly escape made headlines and launched a sensational and long-standing engagement at the Alhambra, a famous London theater and music hall. Each night, he played to a packed house, thrilling British audiences with his seemingly limitless ability to wriggle his way free out of whatever locks and chains they produced for him. Beck had understood that Europe was ready to embrace a man like Harry Houdini, and Harry understood it too. Immediately, he sent for his brother Dash, now an accomplished escape artist in his own right. "Come over," he wired. "The apples are ripe."

LEFT: Harry drummed up publicity in each new city he visited by breaking out of the local jail.

THE KING OF HANDCUFFS

Houdini always refused to say exactly how he was able to open so many shackles so easily. "My brain is the key that sets me free," he would declare when asked. He made no secret of the fact that he had a vast knowledge of locks and handcuffs. He knew some locks had flaws that allowed them to be sprung open if struck in exactly the right place. And it's a safe bet that the "ghost house," the small cabinet in which he actually performed most escapes, safely hidden from the prying eyes of the audience, held a collection of skeleton keys and picklocks, to be used if the need arose.

What Harry understood best was the value of not making the escape look too easy. He always emerged from his ghost house in an exhausted-looking state—with his shirt rumpled and his face glistening with sweat—even if he'd escaped in the first few minutes and had spent the next twenty reading the newspaper or playing solitaire while the anxiety of the audience grew.

LEFT: The King of Handcuffs shows off his muscular build. RIGHT: Four Berlin police officers bind Houdini in cuffs and chains in a poster advertising his appearance at a local circus.

THE GREAT ESCAPES

"It does seem strange," Harry said of his experiences in Europe, "that the people over here . . . fear the police so much. In fact, the police are all mighty, and I am the first man that has ever dared them. That is my success."

It was true that Europeans were more frightened of the police than North Americans were. In many European countries at that time, the police were very powerful, and people had the idea that they could be arrested for the most minor offenses. In places like Germany, France, and Russia, escape acts were popular because they seemed to represent ordinary people getting the better of the authorities. Houdini understood this only too well, and he made it the focus of his act. "I am the greatest of the jail breakers and handcuff kings," he would tell each new audience he faced. "I defy the police departments of the world to hold me."

All over Europe, Harry put his words to the test. In Berlin, he accepted a challenge to try to escape at police headquarters in front of more than three hundred assembled officers. He was stripped naked and secured with handcuffs, leg irons, and thumbscrews. His mouth was sealed with tape—so that if he had a key hidden there, he wouldn't be able to retrieve it. A blanket was thrown over his head to conceal what he was doing. Just six minutes later, he shrugged it off and dropped the shackles to the floor in front of the astonished crowd.

RIGHT: The King of Handcuffs never found a pair of shackles that could hold him.

TOP: A poster of Houdini locked in a jail cell in Amsterdam, just one of many successful prison breaks he made during his tour of Europe.
BOTTOM: Houdini, handcuffed and chained, poses for a magic magazine advert, 1900.

During a tour of Russia, Houdini saw a special prison-transport carriage called a *carette* trundling through the streets of Moscow, and he decided it would become his next great escape attempt. A *carette* was a horse-drawn wagon that was used to transport prisoners to Siberia, a vast, sparsely populated region in the north of Russia. It looked, said Houdini, "very like a safe on wheels," and it was supposed to be impossible to escape from. The *carette* had just one tiny barred window, and its walls were lined with metal to make them impossible to break through.

When Houdini was brought to the Moscow prison where his escape attempt would take place, the secret police hustled him into a back room to be poked and prodded. They combed through his bushy hair, peered into his ears and up his nose, and examined his mouth for hidden keys or tools that might help him escape. "Three secret police, or what we would call spies, searched me one after the other," Houdini later told a friend, "but Mr. Russian Spy found nothing." The *carette* was positioned in the courtyard with its door facing a massive stone wall. As soon as Houdini was shut inside, the police chief told him that he'd locked the door with one key and it could only be unlocked with a second key kept in faraway Siberia. If Houdini was unable to free himself, he'd have to suffer through a brutal, twenty-day journey before he could be released.

Unconcerned, Harry went to work, and within minutes, he was out of the handcuffs and shackles that had bound him. From there, he turned his attention to the floor, sawing through its simple wooden boards using tools that he'd hidden in a hollow metal finger. (For all the care taken during the examination of Houdini, Mr. Russian Spy never spotted the sixth finger on his hand!) In less than an hour, he had escaped the inescapable.

In Europe, Houdini had his first taste of real success. He sold out months-long engagements in every city he visited, and he was earning enough money to take Bess to the best restaurants and to stay with her in the best hotels. Many famous people—from performers and musicians to the Russian royal family—wanted to know him, and he was written about in all the important European newspapers.

In 1902, however, a German newspaper published an article titled "The Exposure of Houdini." In it, Harry was accused of offering a man money to help him fake an escape. According to the paper, Houdini asked the man, a Cologne police officer named Werner Graff, to give him a duplicate key to use during his escape attempt at the Cologne police headquarters. If he was successful, he said, both he and Graff stood to make a lot of money.

Houdini was enraged by the story and hired a lawyer to sue both the newspaper and Graff. At the ensuing trial, Harry argued strongly in his own defense. Graff, he said, had challenged him during one of his performances with a lock he had altered so it couldn't be opened even with a key. When Houdini got free by breaking the lock, a disgruntled Graff made up the bribery story to discredit him.

It must have been quite a scene in the courtroom. Houdini acted almost as his own lawyer, questioning Graff himself and, in his own words, making him swear to "a whole pack of lies." He'd prepared for the trial by working in a local locksmith's shop for ten hours a day, and he came to court with a suitcase filled with locks and handcuffs. "I knew," he later wrote, "that in order to win my lawsuit I would have to open any lock that was placed before me."

And in the end, that is what it came down to. Unable to decide which of the two men was telling the truth, the judge finally asked Houdini if he could escape from Graff's lock without the aid of a key. Houdini said

TOP: Houdini commissioned this poster in order to publicize his win against Graff. It shows Houdini, wrongly accused and handcuffed, as he stands before judge and jury at the Cologne court in 1902. BOTTOM: A rare after-shot of the King of Handcuffs having successfully freed himself from his chains.

DARING DIVE!

This Wednesday, July 15
12:30 P. M. SHARP
BATTERY, NEAR THE AQUARIUM

HARRY
HOUDINI

Now Appearing at Hammerstein's Victoria Theatre and Roof Garden

Securely handcuffed and leg ironed will be placed in a heavy packing case, which will be nailed and roped, then encircled by steel bands, firmly nailed. Two hundred pounds of iron weights will then be lashed to this box containing HOUDINI. The box will then be THROWN INTO THE RIVER. Houdini will undertake to release himself whilst submerged under water.

The Most Marvelous Feat Ever Attempted
in This or Any Other Age.

Wednesday, Rain or Shine

he could, and then moved to a corner of the room, away from prying eyes, to show the judge how he could open it by rapping it on a metal plate he had strapped to his leg beneath his clothes. "What really saved my case," he wrote to a friend, "was that I showed the judge how I opened my cuffs, and that was the best thing I could have done."

Found guilty of slander, Graff was ordered to pay damages to Houdini. And better still, he had to foot the bill for a public apology from the kaiser, which was to be printed in Cologne's major newspapers. The publicity from those printed apologies, and from the trial itself, was priceless.

Houdini's successes in Europe should have paved the way for great things when he finally returned to America. But he'd been away for five years, and others were performing his act as if it were their own. Harry realized that he would have to come up with new and even more daring escapes to leave all his imitators behind.

His first idea was to add an element of danger to his act by jumping off a bridge while handcuffed and chained. Because a stunt like that was tremendously physically demanding, Houdini began training himself to function in extremely cold water and to hold his breath for long periods of time. In the mornings, he would fill a bathtub with water and ice cubes to try to get his body used to the shock of freezing-cold temperatures. Later in the day, he would go for a long run to improve his fitness and increase his lung capacity, until eventually he was able to hold his breath for three full minutes.

Houdini's first bridge escape took place in Detroit in November 1906. Handcuffed, he leaped off the Belle Isle Bridge into the cold, dark waters of the Detroit River. Within minutes, he had freed himself and swum safely back to shore, in what had to be one of his most uneventful escapes ever. But

OPPOSITE: This sequence of images shows Houdini's plunge in April 1908 from the Harvard Bridge into the chilly waters of Boston's Charles River. INSET: A poster promoting another of Houdini's famous dives which took place in 1914 in Battery Park, New York.

31

Taking Flight

One of Houdini's many interests was aviation. In 1903, the Wright Brothers made the first powered flight in Kitty Hawk, North Carolina, and Harry was thrilled by the exciting new era this heralded. During his European tour in 1909, he promptly bought himself a flimsy little biplane he named the *Houdini*.

Aviators were accomplishing new feats all the time, and Harry was desperate to get in on the fun. He knew that several men were vying for the skies, hoping to take flight in Australia, one of the few countries where a first flight had yet to take place. Spotting a chance to be in the history books, he dismantled his tiny plane, packed it in crates, and booked it and himself on a ship bound for Melbourne.

On March 18, 1910, a calm, clear day Down Under, Houdini lifted his biplane off the stony ground below for what was the first officially recorded airplane flight in Australia. "As soon as I was aloft," he said of his historic feat, "all the tension and strain left me. Freedom and exhilaration, that's what it was."

Harry the aviator, 1910.

Houdini was never one to let the facts get in the way of a good story, and when he talked about this escape in later years, he told a much more exciting tale. The river, he claimed, was frozen solid, and a hole had to be cut in the ice so he could enter the water. When he landed, he was disoriented, and then the current pulled him under, so he lost sight of the hole and found himself trapped by the ice. Swimming frantically to and fro, grabbing small breaths from the tiny pocket of air between the water and the ice above, he finally managed to get free. But this was proof, he said, that he really was taking his life into his own hands. "It's only a question of time," he later told a reporter, "that the man who works trained lions and tigers gets his violent passage to the other world, and it is pretty much the same with me."

Audiences were thrilled by these death-defying acts. When Houdini jumped off the Weighlock Bridge in Rochester, New York, ten thousand people turned out to watch. When he jumped off the Seventh Street Bridge in Pittsburgh, there were so many boats on the river below that he hit his head on the bottom of one on his way to the surface and was almost drowned. "I came rushing up at great speed under one of these crafts," he later told reporters. "So rapid was my ascent that in rising I hit my head a fearful blow . . . and sank back into the water again stunned and bleeding. . . . It isn't any fun taking your life in your hands."

It may not have been fun for Houdini, but these escapes were a surefire hit with the crowds. He constantly made them more challenging, freeing himself from piano crates and mailbags and even a giant football. "My chief task," he explained, "has been to conquer fear. When I am stripped and manacled, nailed securely within a weighted packing crate and thrown into the sea . . . it is necessary to preserve absolute serenity of spirit. I have to work with great delicacy and lightning speed. If I grow panicky, I am lost."

One of the greatest of all these death-defying escapes was Houdini's famous Milk Can Escape. In it, he was closed into an airtight metal can filled with water. Volunteers from the audience were asked onto the stage to fasten six padlocks around the rim. Just before he disappeared from view, Harry would invite the audience to hold its breath along with him. As the crowd sucked in a lungful of air, the lid of the milk can was secured, locking Houdini inside, and a curtain was pulled across to hide his labors. Thirty seconds ticked past. Then one minute. Then two. Finally, when three terrifyingly long minutes had gone by and the audience was crying out for his assistant to break open the can with an ax, Houdini would emerge, soaked to the bone but as triumphant as ever.

This escape baffled all who saw it. Many people believed Houdini had supernatural powers that allowed him to rematerialize outside the milk can. Even Bess failed to win ten dollars from her husband when she couldn't tell him how it was done. But in fact, the trick was all in the can. Houdini had it made with false rivets around the neck. Once he was locked inside, he simply pushed up the neck of the can and stepped out, never touching the padlocks at all. Then he waited for the audience to grow anxious before emerging from behind the curtain to accept their relieved applause.

ABOVE: Houdini shows off his famous Milk Can Escape.
BELOW: Harry and his beloved mother, whom he called "an angel on earth in human form."

Houdini's career was more successful than it had ever been. He was invited to tour Europe again and set sail for Hamburg, Germany, on July 6, 1913. Bess remembered what he was like on the pier that day, saying good-bye to his beloved mother. He made quite a sight, she recalled, "clinging to a little old woman in black silk, embracing and kissing her, saying good-bye and going up the gangplank, only to return to embrace her again. . . . She had to order him to go."

The day after Harry and Bess arrived in Europe, a telegram came telling them of his mother's death back in America.

THE LAST ACT

The death of his mother was a devastating blow. Houdini fainted when he heard the news, and he fell into a deep depression that lasted for months. "I who have laughed at terrors of death," he wrote, "who have smilingly leaped from high bridges, received a shock from which I do not think recovery is possible." His mother had been the most important person in his life next to Bess, and now she was gone.

When he finally returned to Europe to complete his tour, after about six weeks of mourning with his family, it was with a heavy heart. "I am working in a sort of mechanical way," he wrote to Dash, "and feel so lonely that I don't know what to do properly." His mother's death had made him think about his own mortality, and perhaps as a result, his escape attempts grew riskier all the time. He freed himself from a straitjacket while hanging upside down from the top of a building, from a crate that was submerged in water, and from a cask that was filled with beer. He even—morbidly— tried escaping from a coffin buried six feet underground.

Houdini's most famous and dramatic escape was called the Chinese Water Torture Cell. Also called the Upside Down, this escape involved a large glass box filled with water. Houdini was locked onto the lid by his ankles and then hoisted over the cell upside down. As the audience watched, he took several deep breaths and then was lowered headfirst into the water. Quickly, the lid was locked in place, and a curtain was

RIGHT: Houdini never failed to escape from the Chinese Water Torture Cell.

pulled around the cell to hide it from view. While an assistant stood by with an ax, ready to break the glass if needed, and the audience looked on in both wonder and fear, Houdini worked feverishly to free himself before his breath ran out.

The Chinese Water Torture Cell was an incredibly difficult trick to prepare and to perform. Even empty, the cell weighed hundreds of pounds, and it took many gallons of water to fill it for each performance. Houdini had to escape within seconds, instead of minutes, because being upside down put extra pressure on his lungs. "I believe it is the climax of all my studies and labors," he said. "Never will I be able to construct anything that will be more dangerous or difficult for me to do." Of all the secrets of his act, this is one of the few he never revealed.

☞ ☜

All these physically demanding and increasingly dangerous escapes were beginning to take a toll on Harry. He was in his forties now, and his body couldn't recover from the stresses and strains of his work as easily as it once did. "I don't know how long this thing can last," he said. "Some time or another we all grow tired. I have been tired for a long time."

He tried to slow down a bit by focusing his stage act more on traditional magic and illusions. He created a trick where he seemed to walk through a brick wall; in another, he made an elephant disappear. Offstage, he started a magazine and wrote several books on magic, and he bought into a store that supplied props to magicians.

By the second decade of the twentieth century, movies were becoming a common and popular form of entertainment, and Houdini

The movies seemed to have been invented just for Houdini. His type of physical entertainment played well on the big screen, and he did most of the stunts himself. But his onscreen exploits—like so many of his escape acts—often put him in genuine physical danger too. ABOVE: Houdini clings to a rock in the onrushing waters of the Niagara River in a scene from *The Man from Beyond.*

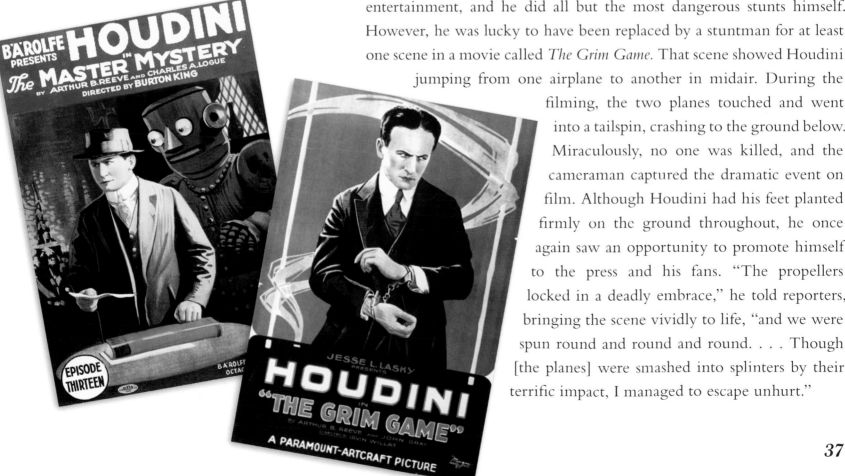

saw in them an opportunity to make himself known to more people in a less strenuous way. His first film, released in 1919, was called *The Master Mystery.* In it, he plays Quentin Locke, a secret agent who goes undercover as a chemist to expose crime and corruption at a shady international corporation. Along the way, he fights off an evil hypnotist, a vicious gangster, and even a murderous robot called the Automaton.

Despite its complicated storyline, *The Master Mystery* was really just a showcase for Houdini's stunts. Audiences watched him escape from an onrushing elevator and from an electric chair. He freed himself from barbed wire just in time to dodge a stream of corrosive acid. Bound with chains and hung from the ceiling by his thumbs, he disabled his captor with his legs and then unlocked the door with his toes.

The movies were tailor-made for Houdini's brand of physical entertainment, and he did all but the most dangerous stunts himself. However, he was lucky to have been replaced by a stuntman for at least one scene in a movie called *The Grim Game.* That scene showed Houdini jumping from one airplane to another in midair. During the filming, the two planes touched and went into a tailspin, crashing to the ground below. Miraculously, no one was killed, and the cameraman captured the dramatic event on film. Although Houdini had his feet planted firmly on the ground throughout, he once again saw an opportunity to promote himself to the press and his fans. "The propellers locked in a deadly embrace," he told reporters, bringing the scene vividly to life, "and we were spun round and round and round. . . . Though [the planes] were smashed into splinters by their terrific impact, I managed to escape unhurt."

ABOVE: This poster advertises Houdini's 1926 tour, which was dedicated to exposing spiritualists as fraud. BELOW: A crowd of children attend Houdini's exposé of spiritualists, 1925.

Houdini was making more money and enjoying greater fame than ever. But all this success had not eased the sting of losing his mother years before. When he was approached by his friend Sir Arthur Conan Doyle, the author of the Sherlock Holmes mysteries, and invited to attend a séance to contact his mother's ghost, he quickly agreed.

Harry missed his mother so much that he was willing to try anything to communicate with her again, even though he didn't really believe in ghosts. He went to the séance with an open mind and tried not to look skeptical as Doyle's wife, acting as the medium, prepared to receive messages from Cecilia Weiss. Soon, Lady Doyle's hand was flying across the pad in front of her, filling the pages with writing from Harry's mother. He didn't say anything to the Doyles after the séance was over, but he knew right then that it was all fakery. The message was in English, a language his mother didn't speak, and no reference was made to the fact that that day was her birthday.

Harry made many other visits to mediums and psychics to try to contact his mother's spirit, but he always came away disappointed. He felt angry that people were being deceived, and he began to attend séances in disguise, so he could expose the mediums on the spot. In 1924, he joined forces with *Scientific American* magazine, which was offering a cash prize to any medium who could prove that his or her methods were real. "I am prepared to reproduce any signal or bit of legerdemain [sleight of hand] they use," he declared, "no matter how unearthly it may seem to the untrained observer."

The front-runner for the *Scientific American* prize was a Boston psychic known as Margery. Margery would deliver messages from the spirit world by channeling her dead brother, Walter. During her séances, all kinds of unexplainable things would happen—tables would

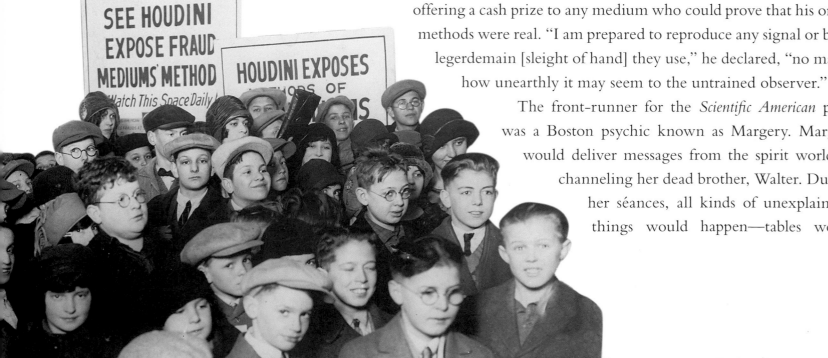

Harry often attended séances in disguise.

slide about and lift up on two legs, bells would ring, the lights would flicker on and off, and Margery would address her guests in the deep, rough voice of Walter.

Of course, Houdini didn't buy any of it, and he was determined to expose Margery as a fraud. He sat in on her séances and found that she was using her own head to lift the table and her toes to ring the bell. To him, she was an obvious con artist. Soon the other members of the *Scientific American* judging committee were convinced as well, and Margery was denied the prize.

"It takes a flimflammer to catch a flimflammer," Houdini said of the *Scientific American* contest. It had left him more convinced than ever that genuine spirit mediums did not exist. He spent a small fortune investigating their claims, and he published a book called *A Magician Among the Spirits*, in which he revealed many of their most common secrets. This made him the focus of threats from spiritualists who were unhappy with what he was doing. "I had a slight premonition," he told a friend, explaining why he'd rushed his book to press, "that perhaps I would not live to see the book in print if I waited much longer."

IT TAKES A FLIMFLAMMER...

Early in his career, Harry had worked briefly as a spirit medium himself, pretending to deliver messages from the dead. He'd read books about mediums and had learned their most common tricks, and he and Bess used these to fool people into thinking they were communicating with their lost loved ones. They even developed a special code to pass information to each other during their act.

Their shows were very popular, but the idea that he was lying to people consumed by grief didn't sit right with him, and he stopped. "I saw and felt that the audience believed in me," he said. "They believed that my tricks were true communications from those dear dead. . . . I was chagrined that I should ever have been guilty of such frivolity, and for the first time realized that it bordered on crime."

Houdini showing how he could ring a bell with his toes without arousing suspicion.

Family Ties

Harry was almost obsessively devoted to his mother. But he was also very close to his siblings. In addition to the five boys Cecilia Weiss brought with her from Hungary in 1878, she and her husband had two more children in America: another son, Leo, born in 1879, and finally the longed-for daughter, Gladys, born in 1882.

Sadly, Harry's half brother, Armin, died from tuberculosis when he was just twenty-two, a loss that deeply affected eleven-year-old Harry. That same disease, which was so common in nineteenth- and early-twentieth-century America, also plagued Nat, a businessman, and Bill, an accountant, throughout their lives. Gladys had struggles of her own after an accident left her with eyesight so poor that she was almost blind. The most successful siblings were Leo, who ran a booming medical practice in New York City, and of course Dash, who followed in Harry's footsteps.

Family was very important to Harry, and it was one of the great disappointments of his life that he and Bess were never able to have children of their own. Still, his love of family was a tremendous driving force, and it pushed him to accomplish great things. "In our journey through life," he once wrote to Bess, "we ought to keep our dear ones in mind all the time."

ABOVE: The five surviving Weiss brothers in 1914. Harry (center) is surrounded by, from left to right, Leo, Dash, Bill, and Nat. RIGHT: Houdini at the grave of his mother in Queens, New York.

In September 1926, Houdini set off on a five-month tour with a show that was less about magic and more about exposing as many spiritualists as he could. During a stop at McGill University in Montreal, he was approached by a student who asked if it was true that he could take any punch to the stomach, no matter how hard. Houdini said it was, and almost before he knew what was happening, the student had delivered three blows in quick succession.

As he got ready for his show that night, Houdini began to feel weak and tired. By the time he'd arrived in Detroit the next day, he was feverish and in severe pain. He insisted on carrying on with his show that night, but he collapsed backstage during the intermission and finished his act only with the help of an assistant. His condition continued to deteriorate, and he was rushed to the hospital in the middle of the night. Doctors operated the next day and found his appendix had burst—a situation possibly aggravated by the blows to his abdomen. A ruptured appendix was a very serious ailment in those days, and in Houdini's case, a severe infection had set in.

Houdini fought hard to survive, but finally—with his beloved Bess, his brothers Dash and Nat, and his sister, Gladys, at his bedside—he said he'd had enough, closed his eyes, and was gone.

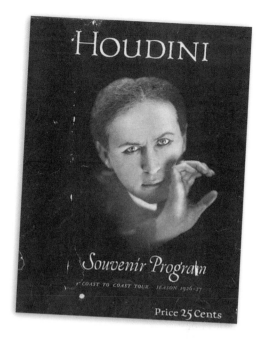

ABOVE: The program from Houdini's final tour of shows. BELOW: Houdini on a park bench in Nice, during his tour of France.

EPILOGUE

Houdini died on Halloween in 1926.

In a strange and slightly morbid turn of events, the bronze coffin he'd had made for his Buried Alive escape was now used to transport his body back home to New York.

Thousands of people packed the hall where his funeral was held, and thousands more lined the streets of New York to watch his funeral procession. Many people had believed that Houdini actually had magical powers, and it was a shock for them to realize that he was just a man after all.

Questions were raised about the circumstances of his death. Some doctors said that the blows to his abdomen could not have caused his appendix to burst, and others were suspicious of the treatment he had received at the hospital in Detroit. Many of Houdini's friends believed the spiritualists he'd gone to such lengths to expose had had a hand in his death, and for eighty-five years, the idea that he was somehow murdered has persisted.

Contrary to newspaper claims that he took his secrets to his grave, Houdini in fact left all his props and magic equipment, as well as many of his most important papers, to his brother Dash, who was known professionally as Hardeen. Dash continued to tour for years, doing some of his brother's most famous escape acts and keeping his name alive.

Bess, of course, was devastated by her husband's death and said that

RIGHT: Good night, Harry.

Helpful Hints for Young Magicians Under Eighty

Throughout his life, Harry loved to give tips and career advice to his fellow wonder workers, especially those just starting out. In his piece, "Helpful Hints for Young Magicians Under Eighty," Houdini shared some of his favorite tips for young magicians. These included the following:

- In winning your audience, remember that "Manners make fortunes," so don't be impertinent.
- An old trick done well is far better than a new trick with no effect.
- Never tell the audience how good you are; they will soon find that out for themselves.
- Well-chosen remarks on topics of the day are always in order.
- An old trick in a new dress is always a pleasant change.
- Always have a short sentence ready in case a trick should go wrong. One magician, who has the misfortune to blunder often, says, "Ladies and gentlemen, mistakes will happen, and that is one of them."
- Rabbit tricks are a positive success.

Houdini and the lovely Jennie, his fabulous disappearing elephant.

"the world will never know what I have lost." Although Houdini had spent years proving that the dead could not send messages to the living, he'd also promised his beloved wife that he would contact her from beyond if he could. They even worked out a secret code so Bess would know if a message she received was genuine. Every year on the anniversary of his death, she invited friends and mediums to gather for a séance, but every year, the prearranged message failed to come. Finally, after ten years, she gave up. "My last hope is gone," she declared then. "I do not believe that Houdini can come back to me—or to anyone. . . . I now, reverently, turn out the light. It is finished. Good night, Harry!"

☞ ☜

Houdini was much more than a magician. He made the impossible seem possible, and in doing so, he made people believe they could accomplish anything they set their minds to. And he proved it in his own life. Despite his humble beginnings, he became one of the wealthiest and most successful entertainers of his day. He faithfully looked after those he loved, and he encouraged those who wanted to follow in his footsteps. He always pushed himself to try new and more daring things, never allowing fear to get the better of him. "The mind," he always said, "is the force that moves the world."

Nothing up his sleeves! The classic image of the world's greatest escape artist.

RESOURCES AND REFERENCES

There are many good books and websites about the life and magic of Harry Houdini. Those who would like to know more should start with the following.

Books

Carlson, Laurie. *Harry Houdini for Kids: His Life and Adventures with 21 Magic Tricks and Illusions*. Chicago: Chicago Review Press, 2009.

Cobb, Vicki. *Harry Houdini: A Photographic Story of a Life*. New York: DK Publishing, 2005.

Fleischman, Sid. *Escape! The Story of the Great Houdini*. New York: HarperCollins, 2006.

Houdini, Harry. *Harry Houdini on Deception*. Edited by Derren Brown. London: Hesperus Press, 2009.

———. *Houdini on Magic*. Edited by Walter B. Gibson and Morris N. Young. New York: Dover, 1953.

———. *A Magician Among the Spirits*. New York: Arno Press, 1972.

———. *Miracle Mongers and Their Methods: A Complete Exposé*. New York: Dutton, 1920.

———. *The Right Way to Do Wrong: An Exposé of Successful Criminals*. New York: Cosimo Classics, 2007. Originally published in 1906.

Kalush, William, and Larry Sloman. *The Secret Life of Houdini: The Making of America's First Superhero*. New York: Atria Books, 2006.

MacLeod, Elizabeth. *Harry Houdini: A Magical Life*. Toronto: Kids Can Press, 2005.

Rapaport, Brooke Kamin. *Houdini: Art and Magic*. New Haven: Yale University Press, 2010.

Silverman, Kenneth. *Houdini!!! The Career of Ehrich Weiss*. New York: HarperCollins, 1996.

Websites

AKA Houdini. www.akahoudini.org. An online biographical exhibit prepared by the Outagamie County Historical Society in Appleton, Wisconsin.

Houdini: Art and Magic. www.thejewishmuseum.org/exhibitions/houdini. The website for the exhibition hosted by the Jewish Museum of New York City.

Houdini: A Biographical Chronology. memory.loc.gov/ammem/vshtml/vshchrn.html. An overview of Houdini's life by the Library of Congress. This site includes links to the many photographs and artifacts in the library's American Variety Stage: Vaudeville and Popular Entertainment collection.

Houdini: The Man Behind the Myth. www.pbs.org/wgbh/amex/houdini. The website for the PBS *American Experience* documentary about Houdini.

Houdini Tribute. www.houdinitribute.com. A fansite that includes hundreds of Houdini photographs, as well as video and audio clips and a biography of his life.

Picture Credits

Every effort has been made to correctly attribute all material reproduced in this book. If errors have unwittingly occurred, we will be happy to correct them in future editions.

Art (throughout): iStock International Inc. / Endpapers: Courtesy of Library of Congress

4: Courtesy of Harvard Theatre Collection, Houghton Library, Harvard University

6: (right) Courtesy of the History Museum at the Castle, Appleton, WI / (left) photo courtesy of Harvard Theatre Collection, Houghton Library, Harvard University

7: McManus-Young Collection, courtesy of Library of Congress

8: © Corbis, drawn by AB Shults / © Corbis

9: © Corbis

10: McManus-Young Collection, courtesy of Library of Congress

12: Courtesy of Library of Congress

13 (top) © Corbis / (bottom) McManus-Young Collection, courtesy of Library of Congress

14: © Corbis

15: © Corbis

16: Courtesy of Toronto Public Library

18: All McManus-Young Collection, courtesy of Library of Congress

19: © Corbis

22: (top) © Getty / (bottom) McManus-Young Collection, courtesy of Library of Congress

23: Courtesy of the History Museum at the Castle, Appleton, WI

24: © Corbis

25: © Bridgeman

26: McManus-Young Collection, courtesy of Library of Congress

28: © Getty / © Alamy

29: Courtesy of Toronto Public Library / © Alamy

30: (main) © Corbis / (inset) Courtesy of Library of Congress

31: All courtesy of Library of Congress

32: © Corbis

33: (top) © Getty / (bottom) McManus-Young Collection, courtesy of Library of Congress

34: McManus-Young Collection, courtesy of Library of Congress

36: (top) Both © Getty / (bottom) McManus-Young Collection, courtesy of Library of Congress

37: (top) McManus-Young Collection, courtesy of Library of Congress / (bottom) Both © Alamy

38: Both images courtesy of Library of Congress

39: (top) courtesy of the History Museum at the Castle, Appleton, WI / (bottom) © Mary Evans

40: (left) McManus-Young Collection, courtesy of Library of Congress / (right) © Corbis

41: (top) Library of Congress / (bottom) © Corbis

42: Courtesy of Library of Congress

44: McManus-Young Collection, courtesy of Library of Congress

45: McManus-Young Collection, courtesy of Library of Congress

46: © Mary Evans

47: © Alamy

48: © Corbis

Source Notes

Page 7: "One morning . . . any visible means of support." From "Harry Houdini by Harry Houdini," in *The Magician Annual* (1909–10).

Page 7: "hardships and hunger." Ibid.

Page 7: "I am going to Galveston, Texas, . . . about a year." Postcard in the collection of the Library of Congress.

Page 9: "a great national refuge for immigrants from all lands." *New York Times*, Dec. 23, 1866.

Page 12: "Christmas is coming . . . I'm magic!" Quoted in William Kalush and Larry Sloman, *The Secret Life of Houdini: The Making of America's First Superhero* (New York: Atria Books, 2006), p. 17.

Page 13: "gave the [magic] profession a dignity . . . and my gospel." Harry Houdini, *The Unmasking of Robert-Houdin* (New York: Publishers Printing Co., 1908), p. 7.

Page 13: "I asked nothing more of life . . . adopted the suggestion with enthusiasm." Ibid., p. 7.

Page 19: "a friendly favor." From "Addressing an Audience," in *Houdini on Magic*, edited by Walter B. Gibson and Morris N. Young (New York: Dover, 1953), p. 238.

Page 22: "Don't think that because you perform a trick well . . . world of mystery." Ibid., p. 240.

Page 22: "the biggest sensation in California since the discovery of gold in 1849." From an advertisement in the October 1899 issue of *Mahatma* magazine.

Page 23: "Most of my success in Europe . . . was to break out of jail." Quoted in Kenneth Silverman, *Houdini!!! The Career of Ehrich Weiss* (New York: HarperCollins, 1996), p. 51.

Page 23: "These aren't stage handcuffs . . . I'll go with you." Versions of this story are told in many Houdini biographies, including *The Secret Life of Houdini*, p. 99; Laurie Carlson, *Harry Houdini for Kids: His Life and Adventures with 21 Magic Tricks and Illusions* (Chicago: Chicago Review Press, 2009), p. 54; and Harold Kellock, *Houdini: His Life Story* (New York: Harcourt, Brace & Company, 1928), p. 141.

Page 23: "Come over. The apples are ripe." Quoted in *Houdini!!!*, p. 64.

Page 26: "It does seem strange . . . That is my success." Quoted in *The Secret Life of Houdini*, p. 120.

Page 26: "I am the greatest of the jail breakers . . . to hold me." From "Addressing an Audience," in *Houdini on Magic*, p. 239.

Page 28: "very like a safe on wheels." Quoted in *Harry Houdini for Kids*, p. 59.

Page 28: "Three secret police . . . but Mr. Russian Spy found nothing." Quoted in *The Secret Life of Houdini*, p. 133.

Page 29: "a whole pack of lies." Ibid., p. 123.

Page 29: "I knew . . . open any lock that was placed before me." Ibid., p. 123.

Page 31: "What really saved my case . . . the best thing I could have done." Ibid., pp. 123–24.

Page 32: "As soon as I was aloft . . . Freedom and exhilaration, that's what it was." Quoted in Vicki Cobb, *Harry Houdini: A Photographic Story of a Life* (New York: DK Publishing, 2005), p. 93.

Page 32: "It's only a question of time . . . pretty much the same with me." Quoted in *The Secret Life of Houdini*, p. 189.

Page 32: "I came rushing up at great speed . . . taking your life in your hands." Ibid., pp. 187, 189.

Page 32: "My chief task . . . If I grow panicky, I am lost." Quoted in *Harry Houdini*, p. 88.

Page 33: "clinging to a little old woman in black silk . . . She had to order him to go." Ibid., pp. 104–105.

Page 34: "I who have laughed at terrors of death . . . do not think recovery is possible." Quoted in *Houdini!!!*, p. 181.

Page 34: "I am working . . . don't know what to do properly." Quoted in *The Secret Life of Houdini*, p. 296.

Page 36: "I believe it is the climax . . . more dangerous or difficult for me to do." Quoted in *Harry Houdini*, pp. 96–97.

Page 36: "I don't know how long . . . tired for a long time." Quoted in *Harry Houdini for Kids*, p. 91.

Page 37: "The propellers locked in a deadly embrace . . . managed to escape unhurt." Quoted in *The Secret Life of Houdini*, p. 357.

Page 38: "I am prepared to reproduce . . . the untrained observer." Quoted in *Harry Houdini*, p. 117.

Page 39: "It takes a flimflammer to catch a flimflammer." Ibid.

Page 39: "I had a slight premonition . . . if I waited much longer." Quoted in *The Secret Life of Houdini*, p. 411.

Page 39: "I saw and felt that the audience . . . it bordered on crime." Harry Houdini, *A Magician Among the Spirits* (New York: Arno Press, 1972), p. xi.

Page 40: "In our journey through life . . . all the time." Quoted in *Houdini!!!*, p. 169.

Page 44: "In winning your audience . . . a positive success." From "Helpful Hints for Young Magicians Under Eighty," in *Houdini on Magic*, pp. 241–42.

Page 45: "the world will never know what I have lost." Quoted in *Houdini!!!*, p. 415.

Page 45: "My last hope is gone . . . Good night, Harry!" Quoted in *Harry Houdini for Kids*, p. 132.

Page 45: "The mind is the force that moves the world." Quoted in *The Secret Life of Houdini*, p. 171.

Design and layout:
Amanda Jekums & Sharon Kish
Illustration: Chris Lane
Copy Editor: Lesley Fraser
Production Editor: Kathy Deady
Index: Ruth Pincoe
Production Manager: Brendan Davis
Editorial Director: Zane Kaneps
Publisher-at-large: Malcolm Lester
Publisher: Oliver Salzmann

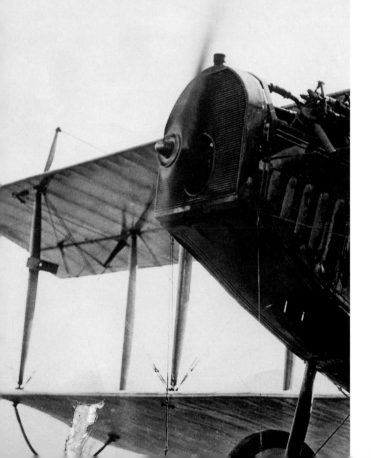

INDEX

I have done things which I rightly could not do, because I said to myself, "You must." –Harry Houdini